PSALMS 23

"The Key to the Cure of all Addictions"

By: *Kevin St. John*

Copyright © 2011 by Kevin St. John

PSALMS 23 "The Key to the Cure of all Addictions"
by Kevin St. John

Printed in the United States of America

ISBN 9781613795460

All rights reserved solely by the author. The author guarantees all contents are original and do not infringe upon the legal rights of any other person or work. No part of this book may be reproduced in any form without the permission of the author. The views expressed in this book are not necessarily those of the publisher.

Unless otherwise indicated, Bible quotations are taken from The New King James Version. Copyright © 1999 by Thomas Nelson, Inc.

www.xulonpress.com

INDEX

DEDICATION vii
INTRODUCTION ix
PSALMS 23 xiii
BRIEF HISTORY xv

CHAPTERS:

   1) ALCOHOL 17
   2) DRUGS 26
   3) FOOD 35
   4) GAMBLING 40
   5) GOSSIP 45
   6) SEX 50
   7) SPENDING 61
   8) THEFT 64
   9) TOBACCO 67
   10) VIOLENCE 72

FINAL THOUGHTS 81

Dedication

This book is dedicated to my Mother who encouraged me to stay away from addictions or destroy addictions. She loved me through all the storms in my life. It is also dedicated to my Lord Jesus Christ who guided me through all those storms.

Introduction

Why is Psalms 23 the Key? The first verse is; "The Lord is my Shepherd; I shall not want." All addictions are selfish wants, not needs. Do not confuse **wants** with needs, desires or dreams. There is nothing wrong with wanting and having nice things. You have a problem when addictions control your spending and physical habits, your physical and mental health, your emotional well being or your soul (your mind, will and emotions). Those are selfish and destructive wants. You and those around you suffer from your addiction. Many have told me over the years "I can handle it.", or "It's not a problem." They have been spiritually blind. In order to completely enjoy the blessings the Lord has for you and the remainder of what David wrote in Psalms 23, you need to become selfless and give your addictions over to the Lord. Addictions are not new and you are not the first to suffer from the oppressive spirit. Many addictions go far back in time. You are special to God, and only you know what you have been through in your life. No one else but you and God, know all your needs, hurts, pains and fears. Just as you do not know what others have been through in their lives? One of the biggest lies of the devil is to make people with addictions believe others have it so easy.

This book is about helping people overcome addictions or avoiding them all together. There has been much said, written and studied on the subject of addictions. I am going to try to simplify each one of these addictions and show how they are not as complicated as people make them to be. The cure may not be that simple to you. Psalms 23 is the <u>Key</u> to the cure! Many topics will be based on my experiences and self education and my pursuit of healthy living.

When you make the Lord your Shepherd you will see things more clearly once you discover the Key. Keep reading and seek the truth in the Word of God that is in the Holy Bible. Sometimes I will paraphrase scriptures. I may not quote or list some scriptures. Quoting chapters and verse numbers of scriptures can sometimes be distracting to the reader. You will find them on your own, when you begin to search for your answers to the cure.

Many people have broken addictions through programs, rehabs, on their own or through false religions. Some have traded them for other addictions or negative behavior. Many people then returned to their addictions. When they return to the addiction it is much worse than before. Anything broken can be repaired. Addictions must be destroyed. Psalms 23 is the key!

Many Christians suffer from addictions because they have never laid their addiction on the altar. Just because some people attend church, or a man or woman of God partakes in something that can be addicting, this does not justify your addiction. There is an old saying that "two wrongs do not make a right".

Let me just say this that "St. John" is just a pen name. My middle name is John & I am a child of God and a saint in God's kingdom. All Christians are children of God and saints, although some denominations do not bestow that title until years after death and much debate. I just like the name for a pen name and do not claim to be perfect. No one but Jesus was perfect, and only He was without sin.

PSALMS 23 *"The Key to the Cure of all Addictions"*

I have overcome some addictions myself and have seen the effects of many addictions while growing up and serving over 25 years in law enforcement. This book is not a replacement for counseling or rehabilitation. At times they can be overrated and very expensive. They are necessary and effective for many people to a degree. For some people it is a waste of time because they play rehab into the cycle of their addiction. Yes, it is your addiction. No one else can claim it, cause it or stop it. You will need help and mostly from the Lord Jesus. This book does not have all the answers. The Word of God in the bible does have all the answers. This book gives you the Key. There are certain substances or circumstances that are gateways to deeper addictions. This book shows you the Key to the truth. You take the Key and open the door. Once you find the truth you can laugh at the devil, close the gate and lock it. Addictions are nothing but lies from the devil. Everyone will be tempted at times in their life. Some people are just partakers and are not addicts, which is possible. Some addictions come on slowly; other addictions may take just one time!

Where is the fine line someone crosses to becoming an addict? "When did this become a problem?" "Why did this happen to me?" "How did I let this get out of control?"

Only the Lord Jesus can fill the imaginary hole in your heart. Trying to fill it with anything else, or any addictions, is like trying to fill a bottomless pit.

If you are still breathing, God has a plan for you. I hope and pray you become encouraged to seek the truth while reading this book and find your answer. The answers to addictions are truly in the Word of God in the Holy Bible and Psalms 23 is the Key! <u>*The Lord is my Shepherd*</u>; <u>I shall not want</u>......

Read on and learn. If you skip to the chapter with your addiction, remember to read all the other chapters. It may help you avoid another addiction and/or you may help someone else with their addiction. May God Bless You!

Kevin St. John

PSALMS 23

1 The LORD *is* my shepherd;
I shall not want.
2 He makes me to lie down in green pastures;
He leads me beside the still waters.
3 He restores my soul;
He leads me in the paths of righteousness
For His name's sake.

4 Yea, though I walk through the valley
of the shadow of death,
I will fear no evil;
For You *are* with me;
Your rod and Your staff, they comfort me.

5 You prepare a table before me in the
presence of my enemies;
You anoint my head with oil;
My cup runs over.
6 Surely goodness and mercy shall follow me
All the days of my life;
And I will dwell in the house of the LORD
Forever.

(NEW KING JAMES VERSION)
BibleGateway.com
Thomas Nelson, Inc.

ABOUT PSALMS 23

Psalms 23 is in the Holy Bible in the Old Testament. Psalms 23 was written by David before Jesus walked on earth. Jesus came to earth later to fulfill scripture and make the New Covenant. Jesus was, in the beginning, with the father. In Genesis 1:26, "Then God said, Let Us….." In John 8:58, Jesus said to them, *"Most assuredly, I say to you, before Abraham was, I AM."* In John 14:6, Jesus said to him, "I am the way, the truth, and the life. No one comes to the Father except through Me." So the Lord, in Psalms 23, is God the Father, Jesus the Son, and the Holy Spirit. Many believe in only God the Father and believe in other gods. If you believe there is not a God then you are making yourself a god. Many believe Jesus was only a great man, teacher, prophet, and messenger. They do not believe that he was the Son of God. This belief is a contradiction in itself: it is not possible because Jesus taught and claimed to be the Son of God. How could a liar be a great man, teacher, prophet, and messenger? The devil is the father of all lies. Jesus is the truth and said in John 8:32, *"And you shall know the truth, and the truth shall make you free."* Psalms 23 is a guide or a map to the future of Jesus being the Lord of Lords & the King of Kings. Psalms 23 is a key. Continue to read and learn more about destroying addictions.

1

ALCOHOL

Alcohol is a drug! Alcohol is a toxin (Intoxicated). Alcohol is addictive. It is available from many different sources and comes in many different forms. It is normally easy to obtain, and its use can start at an early age. *The drug industry is based on greed*, so it would be true to say the alcohol industry is also based on greed. Companies purify alcohol to eliminate <u>most</u> toxins. There are still a small amount of toxins remaining. Alcohol is not healthy. There are claims that small amounts of alcohol are good for your health. The problems far outweigh the benefits. Alcohol affects your mind and body to some degree, no matter how little you use. The alcohol industry is not truly concerned for your safety. They want your money. They are nothing but legal drug dealers. They put out public service announcements to educate the buyer. "Drink Responsibly"; is that possible? They spend billions on cute and sexy commercials. They use foolish actors, animals, reptiles, cartoons, celebrities, and athletes to entice you to buy their product. *They claim they do not advertise to teenagers, which is a large percentage of their business.*

PSALMS 23 "The Key to the Cure of all Addictions"

They lead people to believe that to have fun you have to drink alcohol. Alcohol impairs, inebriates, and intoxicates your mind and body. It blurs your present reality. It can make you temporarily forget things. It enables you to mourn your past. It clouds your future.

Many do not have an alcohol problem now, or they are in denial. *Where is the fine line someone crosses to becoming an addict?* *"When did this become a problem?"* *"Why did this happen to me?"* *"How did I let this get out of control?"* Many say, "It is legal, so I can do it." or "I don't do drugs." They continue to drown themselves in their bottle, cry in their beer or attempt to fill the emptiness in their hearts with alcohol. The media glamorizes it. The world embraces it as a normal part of life and a way to have fun. It is a perfect drug for the sports fan (fanatic). That is why there are so many advertisements during spectator sports. You can have fun and enjoy life and sports without alcohol!

Many parents today still allow underage children to drink at home or home parties, thinking at least they are safe and not doing drugs. This is the epitome of an ignorant and irresponsible parent. Many adults in authority ignore it because they have a problem with alcohol themselves. Some law enforcement officers turn a blind eye to enforcing the alcohol laws. There is a time for discretion, giving certain first-time offenders breaks or taking juveniles involved with alcohol home to their parents. Lax law enforcement, lack of teen education about alcohol and poor parenting skills have kept our youth from learning of the dangers of alcohol.

Now the tides are turning in the United States to go backwards and allow 18 year olds to legally drink alcohol. When I was a teen in Erie, Pennsylvania during the 1970's the drinking age was 21 years old. New York State was 30 miles away where the drinking age was 18. This was before the nationwide law changes were enacted. Alcohol was very easy to obtain, and that is when I first began to see my father and friend's alcohol problems. My drinking was not yet a problem, or so I thought. Some of the things we did and survived are amazing. When young people hear these type stories don't use it as a green light to abuse alcohol.

On "Senior Skip Day" in high school, when I arrived at the beach on Lake Erie, the police had already been there and confiscated the beer keg. At the time, I was disappointed that there was not any beer, because skipping class, smoking, and drinking were a normal thing for me. But there was some feeling of relief of not drinking beer that day because of the long hitchhike back in the rain. Looking back to that day, from my adult life and my law enforcement career, I can see it was a good thing what happen that day. It may have saved my life or that of one of my class mates.

I never drank very much alcohol as an adult. In 2000, I had to stop because of medication prescribed for an arthritic condition. This would later be a blessing, because I went through a divorce in 2002, and I may have turned to alcohol for solace.

As a police officer, I poured lots of alcohol out when found in possession of underage people but I never drank a drop of any confiscated alcohol. Law Enforcement has to contend with alcohol problems every day. Alcohol is a major problem around the world and in some countries it is ignored as a public safety issue. Driving under the influence (DUI) of alcohol or driving while intoxicated (DWI), is the most committed violent crime every day. There are many law enforcement officers around the world who strictly enforce the driving under the influence (DUI or DWI) laws. As long as there are bars, clubs or establishments that serve primarily alcohol beverages, then you will have people that drive after consuming alcohol. If you regularly drive a vehicle under the influence of alcohol then you probably have an addiction. Some law enforcement officers are experts in DUI enforcement and take pride in "getting them off the road." Thank

PSALMS 23 "The Key to the Cure of all Addictions"

the Lord for them. Most of the time, law enforcement is an unseen and a thankless job.

Having worked the late night shift for most of the 90's, I observed many violators who woke up the next morning in jail to face their problem. Some violators even thanked the officers at court. The strict enforcement of DUI laws helped break their addiction, although many violators return to their addiction. Many blame someone else. Some people will feel sorry for them self, and use self-pity to continue their addiction.

There are great organizations that advocate strict alcohol laws and enforcement. Many have signs or television commercials that are very educational. One problem is the "Don't drive drunk" slogan. This causes confusion to some people and is used as a justification. Every one's level of feeling or being drunk is different. Some people may not feel drunk, but they are way over the legal blood alcohol count (BAC) to be operating a motor vehicle. Many people have been injured or killed in vehicle wrecks involving a driver who was under the influence of alcohol.

Continually frequenting places that serve alcohol beverages can lead into an addiction at some point. Never think for a moment that you can hang out at bars or clubs after you stop drinking alcohol in your attempt to destroy your addiction. You need to change your environment. Do not be deceived, ungodly company corrupts good habits. The world constantly bombards people with alcohol advertisements.

Years ago a vehicle wreck involving alcohol was considered a tragic accident by most people. Most people now consider it a violent criminal act and expect justice. There are many people who drink alcohol and never drive a vehicle, who believe they do not have a problem. "I was not driving", is one of their favorite sayings when confronted by law enforcement out in public or as a passenger in a vehicle.

PSALMS 23 "The Key to the Cure of all Addictions"

There are so many social problems associated with alcohol. Alcohol addiction breaks down the family unit and opens the door to demonic activity in the home. It shortens tempers, and it leads to much arguing and domestic violence and many forms of abuse. It causes numerous health problems. It actually lowers your sex drive and performance. It is considered a gateway drug and can lead to other addictions. Gambling, tobacco, illegal drugs and sex addictions are common among people addicted to alcohol.

The new trend is that people who stop drinking alcohol become addicted to prescription drugs. Some people addicted to alcohol will not take medicine. They self-medicate with alcohol and, then say "I am not a pill popper."

There are many organizations treating alcohol addictions with great success. One of the big problems with some group meetings, is they sit around smoking cigarettes and drinking coffee excessively. Both are other forms of addictions. Cigarettes and alcohol many times go hand-in- hand. The more addictions you destroy, the better your life will be. Another problem is some terms, titles or labels associated with alcohol addictions can cause people to continue their alcohol addiction. They will claim it is not in their control. In this book, I do not like to use the term "Alcoholic" and "Alcoholism" because it has been associated with the word "disease". Using these words is like saying some outside force is responsible for your alcohol addiction and that it is beyond your control. Alcohol addiction is a selfish act and is willful misconduct. There are demonic spirits involved with your addiction and there are generational curses within certain people, families and cultures that increase the likelihood of addictions. You have to destroy these curses and addictions with the help of the Lord.

One further note on alcohol addiction meetings: romantic relationships should be avoided with people you meet at these types of meetings. Most organizations will advise this, and most relationships started from these type meetings do not last and cause people to return to their addiction. Also, due to codependency issues, these relationships are at a greater risk of being dysfunctional, if they do last.

Now the <u>Key</u> to you addiction is in Psalms 23. When, "The Lord is my shepherd; I shall not want...." becomes part of your life, then you are on the right path. How do you let the Lord be your shepherd? First accept Him into your heart.

Go now to the "Final Thoughts" section after the last chapter. Then read the sinner's prayer and make the Lord your Shepherd!

Read Proverbs, Psalms and the Gospels of Matthew, Mark, Luke and John and the book of Acts. Concentrate on the red letters which are Jesus quotes, in the New Testament.

Find and attend a Holy Spirit-filled church. You will know it when you find it. Listen to His Word that is taught at church, on television or on tapes/digital recordings. The Lord will never leave you nor forsake you; people, family, friends and co-workers will.

The Lord may have been with you in places you should not have been during your addiction, but his hand of protection may not have been there. I consider this as a sheep going into a cave: the Shepherd may not be able to reach you there. Psalms 23:4 says "Yea, though I walk through the valley of the shadow of death, I will fear no evil; for You are with me; Your rod and Your staff, they comfort me." If you are in the midst of an alcohol addiction, then you are flirting with disaster, or even possibly your eternity. This may not be a "happy hour" thought but it is reality.

With young people, alcohol use increases the chance for many types of accidents due to the increase of risky behavior. Teens can and do become addicted to alcohol. There are many life-long disabilities caused from accidents while using alcohol, all different types of accidents, not only automobile accidents. Alcohol use increases the chance of sexual assault for young women and teens. There is a lot of peer pressure to drink alcohol during High School and College school years.

Many parents send their children off to college only to have a big mess, because they never addressed the issue of alcohol. Some young people used alcohol while at home or were never in any trouble and the parents ignored it. Sometimes young people do not listen and have to learn for themselves, with serious consequences. Just because many before you have done it and survived, this does not guarantee anyone a safe time. Parents who send their children off to college and say, "They need to sow their wild oats" may regret those words. Having worked in a college town for 25 years there have been many lives changed, broken or ruined from alcohol.

The U.S. Military personnel were not allowed to drink in Iraq during Operation Iraqi Freedom. This order has saved our country and military leaders from many problems. This should be done all over the world where the military is stationed. Many crimes, incidents or situations involving the military and alcohol have caused us national embarrassments. Alcohol addictions have been addressed in the military over the years, but not to the extent that they need to be.

Alcohol addictions bring on generational demonic spiritual curses. This is not said as an excuse for an addiction. My father's side of the family was Irish/Catholic. I grew up believing you consumed alcohol beverages at every occasion. There is a very well-known Irish family who made a fortune and was involved in the alcohol industry. They brought forth many public leaders in the United States, but have had numerous tragedies, which I believe are from generational curses that have never been dealt with or destroyed.

The use of alcohol in your home can open a door for demonic activity. Alcohol addictions and curses can be destroyed. Keeping alcohol out of the home is one of the best ways to start.

Remember that Alcohol is a gateway drug and it can open the gate to more serious and harsher drugs. Many drug addicts told me they would have never used harder drugs if they had not used Alcohol, Marihuana and Cigarettes first!

The Lord will not do what you can do for yourself. You have to take the key and lock the gate and with the help of the Lord destroy the addiction. The same key opens your heart to let the Lord inside to be your Shepherd, Savior, Deliverer, Healer, Provider and much more. You have to seek out scriptures in the Bible that pertain to you. Then you use those scriptures as ammunition when temptation comes at you. You can find them by using references, indexes or concordances for the Bible. Find a version you understand and cross reference your favorite scriptures to other versions. Then listen to the Word of God from Holy Spirit-filled pastors at a church, on Christian radio and television, or on tapes, CD or DVD's, or the internet. Faith comes by hearing and you can receive a new revelation every time you hear or read the Word of God.

Prohibition of alcohol was a constitutional amendment. When they repealed the amendment in 1933 it was said to put an end to the black market, corruption and mobsters. In time the mobsters only turned to other black markets: illegal drugs, pornography, prostitution and gambling, to name a few. This contributed to the moral decay of the U.S. which exploded during the 1960's and 1970's. This decay continues to the present date. I believe it has brought a demonic curse upon the United States. The devil and illegal drug industry thrives on the concept that alcohol is legal. In the Bible, Jesus turned water into wine and many people use this one scripture to justify alcohol addictions.

The curse can be destroyed through Jesus Christ. Many people have broken the curses off themselves and their family by accepting The Lord as their Shepherd. They have repented and turned away from their addictions. Maybe you see people who go to church who are addicted to alcohol. That is their problem. Is the use of alcohol beverages a sin? That is between you and God. Do not take anything written here as being judgmental.

This information is for destroying an alcohol addiction or avoiding it. You will kneel in front of the Lord one day and answer to Him for yourself. Do you really want to take the chance of the Lord saying to you "Depart from me I never knew you."? There will be no alcohol in heaven because there is no pain or sorrow in heaven!

(Final Note) In August, 2009, there was a report that 700,000 people die each year from alcohol-related problems in Russia. Alcohol is a tremendous worldwide problem. Psalms 23 as the key to the cure applies anywhere in the world.

2

DRUGS

It is difficult where to even begin on this topic. There are basically two categories of addictive drugs we will discuss in this book. This can vary from country to country. There are illegal street drugs and legal prescription drugs. Some drugs have crossed over into both categories. Let us start with illegal drugs.

Illegal Drugs

Marihuana is for the most part illegal in the civilized world. There has been a major push over the years to legalize it for recreational use or for medical use in the United States. No medical drug that is delivered by inhaling smoke with many toxins is healthy or wise. Just because Marihuana is natural does not make it healthy to smoke or ingest. Put your trust in the Lord for healing not Marihuana.

Remember that Marihuana is a gateway drug and can open the gate to more serious and harsher drugs. Many drug addicts told me they would have never used harder drugs if they had not used Alcohol, Marihuana and Cigarettes first!

Marihuana may not be physically addictive but can be mentally addictive. Marihuana use creates a craving, is habit forming, has ruined countless lives, and has caused people to try harder drugs. Marihuana use does not always lead to people to try harder drugs. Some justify their Marihuana use by saying they do not use harder drugs. By using Marihuana you open demonic activity into your life, family and home. Most people that smoke marihuana also smoke cigarettes. If you are a young person then observe people around 40 - 50 years old who smoke, then people who do not smoke and stay healthy. Then choose how you want to look when you are older.

Marihuana is easy to grow and a very profitable cash crop. The problem is that if the Lord is your Shepherd then the activity of growing, selling or using Marihuana is not in your life. There is a scripture in the Bible about causing someone else to stumble. That is something to think about if you have made money from selling Marihuana. If you think that Marihuana is a harmless drug then you are being fooled. You will be in for a surprise when you kneel before the Lord. You may get rich from selling Marihuana, but it will bring demonic curses on you, your family, and your money.

There are many who have said for years that alcohol is legal and is worse than Marihuana, but that is not a good reason or excuse to use or sell Marihuana. Anyone who has ever used Marihuana knows that you are not going to die or go crazy from casual use. Some anti-drugs messages have said you could go crazy after the first use. Knowing that is not true is not a good reason to use Marihuana. Marihuana use causes so many health problems that there are too many to list here. Anyone who uses Marihuana should ask themselves, "Do I want my doctor, surgeon, dentist, airplane pilot, train operator, bus driver, or taxi driver to be using Marihuana while my care is in their hands?"

PSALMS 23 *"The Key to the Cure of all Addictions"*

As a law enforcement officer I would ask many young people "Why should you not smoke marihuana?" All of them would answer "because it is illegal". I would tell them that is not the main reason. The #1 reason not to smoke Marihuana is because it is bad for your health! Just because Marihuana is legal in some places does not make it good for you.

Heroin, Cocaine & Methamphetamine (Meth) are some the most addictive drugs on the planet. They are not new and their addictions have been around for years. Ecstasy and LSD (acid) may not be as addictive as the others but their use is just as dangerous if not more. In the early 1900s there were approximately 20% of people in the United States addicted to Cocaine. Heroin addiction has been around for hundreds of years. Meth has not been around as long but it is not anything new. These addictive spirits have been around and tormenting people for a long time. So you should never think the Lord does not understand what you are dealing with. You are not the first to deal with the addiction. It is a demonic spirit that Jesus has already defeated.

In the past, governments have used Meth on people or military personnel for higher performance levels. It was administered unknowing the dangers and with carelessness. These were very foolish decisions.

Where is the fine line someone crosses to becoming an addict? "When did this become a problem?" "Why did this happen to me?" "How did I let this get out of control?"

Addictions from these addicting drugs and the physical and mental problems from their use are extensive. The best way to avoid an addiction is to resist any temptation to use them. "Just say No" was really a great anti-drug campaign. Do not even try them once. When someone is already addicted "Just say No" is not easy to say.

There are many reports of people addicted to these types of drugs that have reported hallucinations of monsters, evil creatures, horror or demons. I believe this is the

PSALMS 23 "The Key to the Cure of all Addictions"

Lord showing someone a glimpse into the demonic realm or the fourth dimension. That should be a wakeup call to stop using the drug and get help. There are many great rehab programs out there to deal with addictions from these drugs. They should be used if you are lead in that direction by the Lord. If the Lord is your Shepherd you will know if it is the right thing for you. Rehab programs should not be abused just to sit around, rest, and escape punishment until you can run wild again. If you are using it to obtain a better high when you have completed rehab, then obviously you are in the wrong place and with the wrong intentions.

Many great singers and musicians have had their life cut short by drug addictions! We have all seen this.

Musical lyrics should be listened to with caution when dealing with addictions. Many times they play into emotions that tend to encourage or enable the activity of the addiction. Once an addiction has been recognized, then old favorite songs should be avoided.

Only the Lord Jesus can fill the imaginary hole in your heart. Trying to fill it with anything else, or any addictions, is like trying to fill a bottomless pit.

Most important of all is to make the Lord Jesus your Shepherd. You must accept Jesus into your heart. If you return to your addiction, then more spirits than before will replace the first and you will be worse than you were before.

Psalms 23 is not the cure in and of itself: It is the Key to the cure. Reciting Psalms 23 may help resist temptation, but you need more. This book is not saying there is some simple solution to a highly addictive drug.

There is no problem too big for God! When you make the Lord your Shepherd, then the power of these addictive spirits, become less of a problem to you. When a thought comes to your mind, you can say out loud, "I rebuke that spirit in the name of Jesus!" With that, demons must flee, and peace will enter your heart. Jesus said, "You shall know the truth, and the truth will make you free". This information is very powerful in the area of addictions. Destroy the addiction, and you will be freed from the sins that addictions present.

Addicts are usually consumed with selfishness and emotional pain from the past. Addictions from highly addictive illegal drugs cause people to commit many crimes they would not normally do. They also cause many women to commit immoral acts for money to buy their drugs. God has given us a free will, and with this free will comes responsibility. Any drug used for a temporary high is only bringing bigger problems into your life. These will have long term health problems and possibly eternal consequences. You cannot eliminate past emotional pain with drugs. You are in fact adding more pain into your life. If you are dealing with some physical pain and self-medicating with an illegal addictive drug, then you are, not trusting the Lord for your healing but in a drug. Physical pain should be checked by professionals and researched for yourself in this digital age. Endorphins are a natural substance already placed in the body by God. They are more powerful than any pain reliever. They are very effective for many minor problems.

There are enough toxins in this world already. Many toxins that enter the body will mostly will be eliminated with proper nutrition and under normal conditions. There is no logical reason to add more toxins into your body by using illegal drugs which are made under unhealthy or filthy conditions and with dangerous chemicals. Some drugs are cut with other drugs or chemicals for better profits. Anyone manufacturing or selling these drugs are not concerned for your health or life. It is all about greed, and many drug dealers are willing to kill over their greed. If you die, the only thing the drug dealers will care about is the loss of your business and hope they are not connected to your death.

PSALMS 23 "The Key to the Cure of all Addictions"

The Lord may have been with you in places you should not have been during your addiction, but his hand of protection may not have been there. I consider this as a sheep going into a cave: the Shepherd may not be able to reach you there. Psalms 23:4 says "Yea, though I walk through the valley of the shadow of death, I will fear no evil; for You are with me; Your rod and Your staff, they comfort me." If you are in the midst of a drug addiction, then you are flirting with disaster, or even possibly your eternity.

Go now to the "Final Thoughts" section after the last chapter. Then read the sinner's prayer and make the Lord your Shepherd!

Legal prescription drugs

Just because a drug is prescribed by a doctor, or sold at a pharmacy, does not make it safe to abuse. There are many types of pain medications, muscle relaxers, anti-depressant medications and weight loss medications etc... that can be addictive. Most ethical doctors will only prescribe drugs for a certain period of time as needed. Some doctors are careless in prescribing these drugs. Some people scam doctors to get prescriptions for drugs to feed their addictions. Addicts will steal the medication from family, friends, or anywhere possible. Some will buy these drugs on the street from people who steal them, or scam the doctors or pharmacies for them. Many people selling them are doing it to feed their own drug addiction. Generally addictive prescription drugs are easy to get, and therefore have become a part of the illegal drug trade. A legal prescription drug becomes illegal to possess when you do not have a prescription for that drug or when it is sold or transferred to someone without a prescription.

Many youth today steal prescription drugs from parents or relatives. Many young people do not know what drugs they are taking, and this could have deadly consequences.

This is especially true when they are used in combinations or with alcohol.

Some people have their favorite type of prescription drug and abuse it for years thinking that it is a hidden addiction. Since it is legal, than it is ok in their minds. The new thing among reformed alcohol addicts is to be addicted to prescription drugs that provide the same or similar feeling as alcohol. This is trading one addiction for another.

Some people mix pills with alcohol and they can become extremely intoxicated and inebriated. They can be very dangerous to themselves or others. They can lose memory of things that have happened and many people have died using a combination of pills and alcohol. Often abusers think using a combination of pills and alcohol will keep them out of trouble, if they are caught while driving a vehicle, due to having a lower blood alcohol count. Drugs still show up in a blood test. This trick is known by law enforcement and the court system.

Any drug prescribed by a doctor should only be used according to the doctor's instruction, the pharmacy's instruction and with guidance from the Lord. You will know when a drug is not needed anymore during a sickness or healing when the Lord is your Shepherd. There is a big debate among doctors, pharmacists and natural health care experts over some legal prescription and nonprescription medications. What we are talking about in this book, are those drugs which can become addictive. Most people addicted to a legal prescription drug know they are addicted. If someone has been prescribed a legal addictive drug for a long period of time, it would be wise to seek a second opinion from another doctor. In the case of terminal illness that is a different story. If a miracle healing occurs then an addiction can be dealt with then. God can heal both.

To abuse medications has physical, mental and spiritual consequences. Many of the issues described in the illegal drug section apply to addictions involving legal prescription drugs.

Some notes on other drugs or intoxicants:

There are always going to be new drugs discovered. There are many rare drugs out there. There are also lots of chemical inhalants and mood-altering substances that people use for a quick high: Some are used by young people experimenting, or addicts that cannot find their drug of choice.

Only the Lord Jesus can fill the imaginary hole in your heart. Trying to fill it with anything else, or any addictions, is like trying to fill a bottomless pit.

Caffeine

Just a short note on this mild stimulant; There has become a craze worldwide with energy drinks and weight loss pills filled with caffeine. This is affecting people's health to an unknown degree. Tea and coffee have been around for years. I believe in the future they will determine that caffeine is not good for your heart over a long period of time or in excessive amounts. I have been for the most part caffeine free for 8 years and enjoy better sleep and better endurance workouts. Young adults and teens should avoid caffeine and caffeine stoked so called energy drinks in excessive amounts. Adults should monitor their own levels according to their health and discuss the topic with their doctors.

Go now to the "Final Thoughts" section after the last chapter. Then read the sinner's prayer and make the Lord your Shepherd!

Read Proverbs, Psalms and the Gospels of Matthew, Mark, Luke and John and the book of Acts. Concentrate on the red letters which are Jesus quotes, in the New Testament.

The Lord will not do what you can do for yourself. You have to take the key and lock the gate and with the help of the

Lord destroy the addiction. The same key opens your heart to let the Lord inside to be your Shepherd, Savior, Deliverer, Healer, Provider and much more. You have to seek out scriptures in the Bible that pertain to you. Then you use those scriptures as ammunition when temptation comes at you. You can find them by using references, indexes or concordances for the Bible. Find a version you understand and cross reference your favorite scriptures to other versions. Then listen to the Word of God from Holy Spirit-filled pastors at a church, on Christian radio and television, or on tapes, CD or DVD's, or the internet. Faith comes by hearing and you can receive a new revelation every time you hear or read the Word of God.

Recovering drug addicts should not get hung up in the Old Testament or the book of Revelations. These may be too complicated at the beginning of your walk with the Lord and recovery period. In the Bible, the books of Matthew, Mark, Luke and John, then Acts and Proverbs, is where most of your time should be concentrated during the first steps of your walk with the Lord. Remember, Psalms 23 is the Key! "<u>The Lord is my Shepherd</u>; <u>I shall not want</u>..." Take the Key and may God bless you!

3

FOOD

Some men live to eat, some men eat to live. (Socrates, Greek philosopher).

In the last 30 years food has become an obsession in the United States and other parts of the world. Advertisements are everywhere and people are becoming more overweight and obese. There have been many cases of 800 - 1000 pound people. They cannot even leave their homes. There was a news article of an obese woman in Florida who died and her skin had grown into the couch. These obese people must have had someone bringing them food. These are extreme cases, but the point being, someone was enabling them. Most people are enabling themselves. Maybe for a time a parent or guardian encouraged you to eat all your food or have more. They may have unintentionally started your addiction or given you improper nutrition. There comes a time where you are responsible for your own intake of food, and why you eat the amounts you do.

Some foods just taste so good, or they have additives that make you crave them more. Much of the processed food and snack industry have researched and produced great tasting items. Great tasting snacks and addictive food makes these companies more profit.

Some people turn to food to fill their hearts from past emotional and physical abuses. They become depressed, sad, worried, anxious, or lonely. They turn to food to ease their emotional pain.

Only the Lord Jesus can fill the imaginary hole in your heart. Trying to fill it with anything else, or any addictions, is like trying to fill a bottomless pit.

People compare themselves to others and give up on their own personal health. Many people are sitting too much and spend too much time watching the TV, playing video games, or staying on the computer. This is a major problem with the youth today in developed countries. Lots of people are working too much in non-physical jobs, and then stay idle in their off time. Even small amounts of exercise in a day, is better than nothing at all. A short walk or taking the steps instead of the elevator is a form of exercise.

Exercise is not the only solution to this problem. If you have a food addiction then an exercise program will usually last for a short period of time. When little or no results are seen then a "give-it-up mentality" sets in. For most people a diet usually only last for a short period of time. When the craving and addiction returns, the weight returns. The diet industry knows this and is part of the plan to keep customers.

You are what you eat is a very true statement. Next time you walk through a grocery store look at the isles full of nothing but junk food. Sodas are a major problem to people with addictions. An old friend once told me she quit drinking a brand name soda she was addicted to and she lost 60 pounds. That is all she did! She was very attractive lady and much of her youthful beauty was restored.

During my early thirties I began to put on some weight and became sluggish. My wife and I lived near her family café. Sodas and deep fried food were a regular meal for sev-

PSALMS 23 *"The Key to the Cure of all Addictions"*

eral years. I bought a mountain bike and began to watch what I ate. My main goal was to build my endurance and energy. I dropped back down to my normal size in no time at all. I began using weight machines and then later free weights to build muscle along with the endurance from cycling.

There are many great programs for exercising. The ones mentioned worked for me. You need to find the one that works for you. Walking is one of the best and cheapest forms of exercise. Parking farther out at the store or walking up the steps, instead of taking the elevator, may just be the right start for you. The most important muscle you need to exercise is your heart. You do not have to go out like an endurance athlete just to be in good health or good shape.

Whatever you do make it something you enjoy, and keep it a regular part of your life, not a fad. Things may change over time, but keeping moving is the most important part.

After mountain biking for years, I slowly (and reluctantly) changed to road biking. The change has really been good for me. I still keep a regular walking routine during the off season.

In 2007 I rode the Cheaha Challenge, at age 48, for the third time. It was an 88 mile bike ride up the highest point in Alabama, which took 7 hours. This level of fitness did not come overnight for me, nor will it for you. The most important thing is to get started and then stay with it. Still if you do not face your food addiction and continue to take in the same amount of improper food then you will get the same results. If you diet alone, without exercise, most people will return to their food addiction. It is an ongoing "lifestyle change". It is really about being in good physical health. A commitment to a healthy life style must be decided.

When the focus of your life is, "The Lord is my Shepherd, I shall not want.", then when you go to buy food, you will make healthier choices. You will buy the food that you need and not everything you want. There are Christians that are overweight, and they have made bad choices in the past with their eating habits. This is a very sensitive topic with many people. Find out what is best for you in a healthy lifestyle. Do not fall into the "give-it-up mentality. Just because one program or system does not work, then "PUSH" - <u>P</u>ray <u>U</u>ntil <u>S</u>omething <u>H</u>appens.

I do not count calories; buy low fat or diet items. I use real butter and milk. I eat few snack foods. I try to eat some fruit or something healthy for snacks.

Years ago deep fried food was a treat. Something you had just once in awhile. Now it is everywhere and an everyday meal for some people. It is quick, easy, cheap and a tasty food for restaurants to serve. The deep fried foods can be addictive. But make you sluggish, and certainly lead to build-up in your arteries.

We need food to recover from previous use of energy, and to refuel for the future need for energy. Notice the operative word here is "need", not "want".

Many people know the results of overeating but may not care until they see a doctor. Then want the doctor to fix the problem. Unfortunately doctors are not like a mechanics, who can just replace the engine. You have to take the initiative.

I have seen many celebrities on TV promoting diets.

Then a few years later it is reported that they are overweight again. There are many gimmicks on TV with models using some type of exercise equipment. These people did not get into shape on that piece of equipment! A commitment to a healthy life style is more important than any program or piece of exercise equipment.

Many people turn to diet pills to deal with food addiction. They are prescribed or bought over-the-counter. These substances are not good for the heart or body over time. They may also create another addiction to the diet pills. Which have a "speed-like" effect on the body.

PSALMS 23 *"The Key to the Cure of all Addictions"*

There are many "diet" foods or drinks that are not healthy. Be watchful for exaggerations and false claims: take a little time to educate yourself on foods, diet products and exercise equipment.

Many Christians struggle with food addiction. If someone is overweight and fairly healthy, and o.k. with the Lord, then so be it. Their past addiction is not of anyone's business. Maybe they have broken their addiction, but now have to live with the results of it. It is not easy to eliminate body weight, and nothing written here is to make it seem otherwise. When the Lord is your Shepherd, then more than anyone or anything, He can help your overcome your addiction.

4
GAMBLING

This is a multi-billion, if not trillion, dollar industry all over the world. It is condoned by some Christian denominations, and many Christians participate in gambling. Others ignore it. Many governments regulate it, condone it, or even run it. Some think it is harmless entertainment, and will justify it. The money that flows through your hands and how you use it will be judged by God in the end. From a biblical standpoint, gambling your money is not being a good steward of your money.

The words "luck" or "lucky" are nowhere to be found in the bible. If you believe in "good luck" then you believe in "bad luck" which is biblically demonic.

Gambling is all about chances not luck and the chances are very good that you are going to lose! If you win, it is easy to want more or bigger winnings. If you win big it is harder to quit because you think you can do it again. If you lose, most people will want to try to win back their losses.

If you own or run a gambling operation then chances are you will make money, but have many problems with your "winnings". These profits are biblically cursed money and viewed by God as profiting from the loss of others. In essence it is stealing from others. It is very interesting that large gambling operations have to spend vast amounts of money on security to monitor their employees from stealing or making deals with players. These are deals when the employee helps the gambler to win. The employees know how much the operation (house) is taking in, yet deep down they know it is stealing. As the saying goes, "if you will steal for your boss, then you will steal from your boss".

When alcohol was legalized in the U.S., in 1933, it was said that this would help do away with the underworld or mob. But the truth is, the mob just moved into other forms of corruption: gambling was one of them.

In the early 1980's after I got into civilian law enforcement I watched the movie, "Serpico", about illegal gambling and corrupt cops in NYC. I thought that could not really happen, and it was hyped up for a movie. In the 1990's, I watched it again, and thought well maybe that could have happened! In 2008, after retiring from 28 years in law enforcement, and working in Iraq with cops from all over the country, I watched the movie again, and said "That really happened"! Government entities condone gambling through state lotteries and regulation, but at the same time, make it illegal for others to operate. This is hypocritical to many people. Law enforcement's job is protecting the public and this gives an appearance that the government is allowing the state to profit and not others. So for this reason many in law enforcement look at gambling as a little gambling on the side is not all that bad. This attitude is all over the world where gambling is legalized is some form or another. Some politicians use the phrase "You cannot legislate morality." This is a foolish statement, since most of U.S. original laws and constitution are based on biblical principles.

In summation, this book is about addictions, and everyone who gambles is not an addict.

PSALMS 23 *"The Key to the Cure of all Addictions"*

Where is the fine line someone crosses to becoming an addict? "When did this become a problem?" "Why did this happen to me?" "How did I let this get out of control?"

When the "Lord is your Shepherd", and you know this in your heart and believe His Word then you will have no desire to gamble. Jesus talks about money all through the New Testament. Read a bible with Jesus' Words in red letters. Not anywhere will you see where Jesus condones gambling or wasteful spending. Gambling is a means to get something for nothing and is not honest gain. For the rich it is less money to give and for the poor it is less money to live. Governments create a "lottery mentality" which is also part of the mind set in social programs. Many people scam the system to get something for nothing. If gaining from gambling or a scam it is "Easy come and easy go".

In the U.S. it is said that approximately 10% of all money is spent on gambling. This is probably true in other countries as well. It is also probably true that most people do not tithe 10% of their income to the church. Tithing is always a sure bet. Find a church that you feel confident with the leadership and then leave the worries of what is done with the money to God. Will a man rob God in tithes and offerings? You will be more blessed tithing than gambling. I have not lost money since I began tithing, and have been very blessed.

When working in Iraq, guys would ask me to play poker with them. I would tell them, "I cannot afford it". Their reply would be, "you make the same as us, so you can afford it." I would tell them that I make more because of my monthly pension, and I would just leave it at that. Sometimes the best witnessing tool is by example.

Gambling is based on greed and getting something for nothing. It is coveting another person's money. It is a "get-rich-quick" mentality for many, and extremely reckless behavior. It gives people false hopes and takes money from starting new businesses or prospering in other areas or from giving to the needy. There are many stories of how big winners of lotteries have lost everything. Some of these have labeled the money they won as "cursed money".

Alcohol and gambling addictions many times go hand in hand. I once read where everyone was happy flying into a major gambling city that has lots of casinos. Flying out of the city, most people have lost money and are very quiet and sad.

My dad told me "There is a sucker born every day". The sad truth of the matter was he was an alcohol addict and possible a gambling addict. He died living in a mobile home with very little and should have been a multi-millionaire.

I remember as a teen in the mid-1970s going to a Catholic Church bazaar with my dad and older brother one Sunday afternoon in Erie, PA. I was told there would be games and things to win prizes. (My friends and I played poker and drank beer in those days unknown to our parents.) When I walked into this bazaar in the gym, I was shocked to see poker and black jack tables and a roulette wheel. My dad had given me some money prior to arriving, and when we entered he said, "You can only drink one beer". My friend and I could not believe what we were being allowed to do! Thank the Lord I did not make that a normal part of my life.

I have seen many friends in the early stages of gambling addictions, playing the lottery and betting on horse racing. I have read and seen many news articles of the corruption at the horse tract and the Pennsylvania lottery commission, back in my younger days in the 1970s. I thank the Lord that Alabama (my home now), has never has allowed the lottery to this day in 2010.

Christians should not partake in any form of gambling, including investing in ownership or voting to allow it. This brings curses onto you and your family that are not worth the monetary gain for you or your community.

If you are in debt over gambling or have been in the past, then you have an addiction. *There is no problem too big for God! When you make the Lord your Shepherd, then the power of these addictive spirits, become less of a problem to you. When a thought comes to your mind, you can say out loud, "I rebuke that spirit in the name of Jesus!" With that, demons must flee, and peace will enter your heart. Jesus said, "You shall know the truth, and the truth will make you free". This information is very powerful in the area of addictions. Destroy the addiction, and you will be freed from the sins that addictions present.*

The Lord will not do what you can do for yourself. You have to take the key and lock the gate and with the help of the Lord destroy the addiction. The same key opens your heart to let the Lord inside to be your Shepherd, Savior, Deliverer, Healer, Provider and much more. You have to seek out scriptures in the Bible that pertain to you. Then you use those scriptures as ammunition when temptation comes at you. You can find them by using references, indexes or concordances for the Bible. Find a version you understand and cross reference your favorite scriptures to other versions. Then listen to the Word of God from Holy Spirit-filled pastors at a church, on Christian radio and television, or on tapes, CD or DVD's, or the internet. Faith comes by hearing and you can receive a new revelation every time you hear or read the Word of God.

Gambling addictions can cause depression and suicide. Store your treasures up in heaven. That is in the Word of God in the Bible. When the "Lord is your Shepherd" then you will be blessed, in God's time, maybe not in your time. Gambling is just saying to God "I want it now". You may get it now but the curse comes along with it.

Go now to the "Final Thoughts" section after the last chapter. Then read the sinner's prayer and make the Lord your Shepherd!

5

GOSSIP

How can this be an addiction, and is gossip really that harmful? There are many scriptures that address gossip but just do not use the term "gossip". This is why so many people consider it harmless.

There are many television shows that prey on people's addiction to gossip. These shows are about people's personal lives and secrets. This started as day time soap operas in the early years of television, and has since moved into some of the evening television shows. Next the gossip bled into sports news and regular news. Now you have murder operas. Then it came to reality shows. The point about these broadcast shows is that it has fueled many people into craving for more and more gossip. These type television shows are all over the world.

Some people are obsessed with other peoples' business, in their homes, workplaces, schools, churches, and even our government. Gossip has destroyed marriages, careers, educations, ministries, political offices, and torn apart families. Many times gossip only has a saw of truth. Ninety percent is twisted, embellished, or just flat out lies. The story gets bigger and bigger as it goes through the grape vine.

Now there is a difference between gossiping and reporting suspicion of criminal or abusive activity: reporting crimes or other abuse affects the physical safety and welfare of others. In my years of law enforcement, I have encountered people who said that they did not want to get involved by reporting crimes and abuse. They will not report true information to government officials, but ironically, will tell friends and family.

Worrying and talking about other people's marital problems is a waste of time. In my first marriage, I told my ex-wife that I did not want to hear of the neighbor's marital problems, because we had enough problems of our own to last a life time. When rumors are spread about other people's marriage, it only makes their problems compounded and could cause a divorce. This would be considered getting in between what God has joined together. If you hear something, and tell one spouse to spite the other spouse, then you are on dangerous ground in the Lord's eyes. If you could go to one, or the other, in the marriage, and help solve a problem, then that would be better than spreading gossip. If that is not possible, then pray to the Holy Spirit, and let Him deal with it. Then you need to drop the issue. If the Lord is your Shepherd, then the Father and Holy Spirit will hear your prayers. If you sow gossip, then you will reap gossip. That is why many people who spread gossip believe gossip and the cycle continues.

Gossip is not gender specific. Men can be just as addicted to gossip as woman. Many men will use gossip and other "cut-throat" tactics in the workplace to get a promotion or title. They are usually man pleasers, ungodly and spiteful.

Both genders use gossip in the workplace as a means to an end. Many times it will spill over into a person's home life. Most of the time gossip is viewed as counterproductive in the workplace, but many times gossip is tolerated.

People that gossip are usually spiteful, too. If someone speaks up or is a whistle blower to wrong doing or unethical behavior, then the retaliation or revenge usually begins. "Pay back is hell" is a common saying and that may be right. Hell just might be waiting for those who use gossip as revenge.

A young police officer came to me just before I retired, and said that he thought all the childish gossip ended in high school. I told him to hang in there, because it continues all through your career. Gossip permeates from the local level all the way up to the federal level in government work. One thing to remember is that you have to stand accountable to the Lord for every idle word you speak.

Gossip in school is generally understood as childish, but can still cause lifelong scars. Once in the college level it can turn to domestic disputes or violence. The internet has become a tool to spread rumors and gossip among young people. It has caused extreme emotion pain to many. The simple solution is to ignore it, or contact the web masters and have it removed.

Gossip in the church is one of the most destructive spirits coming against the church. When people in church ask you "why" this and "why" that, you know they are just looking for some form of gossip to spread to others. If you need to know why about someone's personal life, they will tell you. Then that should be the end of it, if you are to be trusted. Many people stop attending church because of the gossip they have encountered there. Church is the one place most Christians would least expect to find gossiping: sadly, it happens there too. Let the Pastor or the Holy Spirit deal with it.

When I hear of something negative someone speaks of me, through someone else, I tend to make a joke of it to myself. Some things are just not worthy of a response. You do not have to accept what someone else says, and you do not answer to the Lord for what others say. When you respond, to set the record straight, then it just continues making the problem bigger. You can only be offended if you accept it. At the same time no one should allow themselves to be a door mat. God always has the last word.

Politicians have come under so many attacks due to the rampant corruption in politics. Many of these politicians get on news shows and defend themselves against gossip. Some celebrities and comedians claim to be authorities on political issues and spew there vile out in the form of gossip, opinion and ignorance. Many politicians will use gossip or mud slinging in political campaigns to win a victory. The truth is so blurred in politics today that many people will not even vote in elections anymore. If voters would obtain the facts and not be led by gossip and biased opinions of the news media, then a more informed decision could be made about who to vote for. Political corruption is one thing that should be exposed but making a circus of a politician's personal life or family problems is totally different.

Many families have been torn apart from gossip within the genealogical tree. This has led to family members not speaking, being angry for years, or even domestic violence. Just because it is extended family does not make some issue your business. There is a fine line that some family members should not cross. Prayer and looking to the Lord and His Word, for the answer, is always the best for family issues. If abuse or violence is involved action should be taken immediately and if needed reported to the authorities.

When the Lord is your Shepherd and you read and understand His Word, then you will become less likely to get involved, or even want to know other peoples' business.

There are magazines and tabloid newspapers that are completely dedicated to gossip. They get a few facts straight some times. Just enough true information is written to keep them from being taken to civil court and held liable, or to be sued for defamation of character.

While writing this chapter in November 2009 the news has been full of a famous sports figure's personal life. There was an accident and an incident at his house just days after tabloid news wrote of him having an alleged affair. The news media and many people will be consumed with this for some time. Most of it is of no ones' business. If you got hooked on the good gossip and bought the products then you probably will get sucked into the bad gossip too.

Gossip has been around for years and is in parts of the world where television does not exist. Cell phones are just about everywhere now. A gossip addiction can be destroyed. Read the Bible and be careful of what you speak. We all are held accountable for every idle word we speak. As my Pastor says; "Go to the throne, not to the phone."

6

SEX

S ex is God's given desire and spiritual bond between a man and a woman in marriage. It has become a trillion dollar industry all over the world, and in God's eyes it is not for sale. It has been perverted in every shape, form, and fashion anyone can imagine.

Let me just say this before going further into this chapter. St. John is just a pen name. My middle name is John & I am a child of God and a saint in God's kingdom. All Christians are children of God and saints, although some denominations do not bestow that title until years after death and much debate. I just like the name for a pen name and do not claim to be perfect. No one but Jesus was perfect, and only He was without sin.

Today the immoral and ungodly people attack God's messengers. They will attack anyone who speaks of morality, God, or the Bible. Examples of this are: a beauty contestant spoke out against homosexual marriage, and one of the judges began a vile and vicious attack on the internet towards her; a conservative politician had an affair with a woman in another country and suffered a media attack of his views; a mega church pastor had a drug and homosexual sexual relationship outside of his marriage. The liberal media had to dig deep to find any sin with the beauty contestant. I knew when she spoke out that they would dig until they found some sin to degrade her. The other two brought things upon themselves. The point here is that is does not matter what these three people did, or anyone else for that matter. It does not change the Word of God. You cannot justify immoral behavior by someone else's sin.

Many people will avoid this chapter or critique it to the very end. Too many people are ignorant or in denial of God's Word. Been there, done that, got the divorce. You do not have to be a theologian, professor or a bible expert to understand God's Word concerning sex. Rebellion is the principal that Satan builds his kingdom on and sexual rebellion abounds in our world today.

What is a sexual addiction? We will explore this question. Can a man and woman in a monogamist marriage have sexual addiction? This question may be beyond the author's knowledge and is not really the purpose of this chapter and book. God said "be fruitful and multiply". So we will leave that question to God, the married couple, and possibly a Christian-based professional counselor.

Sex can be like a highly addictive drug. One experience and a craving for more can develop. Most people that are not married have sex more than one time, and most women do not get pregnant from sex one time. Many women get pregnant every day from sex outside of marriage. This often ends in abortion, which is one sin leading to another. Single mothers will many times live with hardship, guilt and shame. Some women and men have multiple sexual partners and have no guilt or shame. They know it is wrong, or sinful, but do not care, they live in rebellion to God's word.

A famous quote of Jesus used by immoral people is, "He who is without sin cast the first stone."! They use this to justify all kinds of sexual sin. The situation Jesus was speaking of was of a woman caught in adultery and fornication. Others were going to stone her to death. Jesus said this to them, because we are not to condemn each other to death or hell for any sexual sin. He will be the judge in the end.

There is a part of the same chapter that immoral people ignore or are ignorant of. It is just a few scriptures past this famous quote. Jesus told the woman "Go and sin no more."! She was caught in the act, exposed, and now knew what she had done was sin. There were not any more excuses for her now. Jesus was not telling her to be perfect. He was telling her not to continue committing sexual sin any more. When someone tells you or convicts you of sexual sin it is not condemnation. It may be the Lord speaking through them for you to "Go and sin no more." You can spend your whole life saying to people "Do not judge me." but in the end, you will bow to Jesus and answer for your sins. This includes all people of all races and religions. Let the Lord worry about those people, who have not had His Word properly spoken to them, or the Word has not reached them. Those people who pervert the Word of God to commit sexual sin will answer to Him in the end.

Fornication is normally known as sexual relations outside of marriage. It can be with one partner or multiple partners. Many men and woman live together, or have sex together, prior to marriage. They get started and a craving begins. Is this an addiction? Many people never get married, even if there is a hope or promise to marry before sexual relations begin. Many people do marry after having sex, but carry the sin into their marriage. Some men have even used the excuse that they fornicated with their wife prior to marriage as justification to commit adultery while they are married. Sexual sin prior to marriage needs to be addressed if you are now married with prayer and asking God for forgiveness.

Many people living together believe they have a monogamous relationship. Some do have a good relationship, but it

PSALMS 23 "The Key to the Cure of all Addictions"

is still sin. Others just change the rules, because they made the rules themselves. Is sexual sin an addiction? Are all these situations mild or major forms of addiction?

New Age religion is having no religion, but putting yourself in the middle of your world instead of God and making yourself a god. Other than new age, there are many liberal people's views on sexual sins at this time. The Bible is clear on them, and some just ignore it, or twist the Word of God in the Bible around to justify their sin.

Sexual sin leads to divorce, jealousy, sexually transmitted disease, assault, murder, and abortion. Abortion is a form of murder. There is no such thing as prochoice. Abortion has become a way of covering sexual sin and sexual addiction in our world. Abortion is not an option in God's eyes. I am not condemning anyone for their past sins but once you read this, and God's Word, and believe it is a sin, then there is no justification to have an abortion. Jesus said "Go and sin no more."! Repenting from sin just means turning away and moving away from it, and back towards God. God wants for you to have the best sexual relations, inside of marriage and between one man and one woman!

Fornication runs the major risk of acquiring sexually transmitted diseases (STD's). Some have preached that God is punishing fornicators, homosexuals, or immoral people with STD's. This is false preaching: God does not give anyone a spirit of infirmity. These STD's / "spirits" are from the devil. There is a price to pay after all immoral pleasures. God's hand of protection may not be with you if you are living outside His will. Give your life to the Lord and get in His will. You can be healed if you are already infected. If not in this life then healing is for sure in the next life.

Between STD's and abortions there are enough statistics to show that the risks are very high of having physical or emotional problems from sexual relations outside of marriage. A new thing among many young people is they believe

PSALMS 23 "The Key to the Cure of all Addictions"

that sex without intercourse is not sex. You will not get pregnant, but still risk the chance of STD's, and are still playing with fire. Is fornication a form of sexual addiction? Sin is still sin.

Adultery is having sex when one or both persons are married, but not to each other. "Thou Shall not commit Adultery" is one of the Ten Commandments in the Bible. This must be very important to God or it would not be there. If fornication is not a sin, then why would God include this in the Ten Commandments? If sex is not a big deal outside of marriage, then why would it be a big deal in marriage? I have two sayings about adultery; (1) "It is all about proximity." and (2) "flirtation leads to teasing, and teasing leads to sin."!

Please do not debunk this whole chapter, or book, or the Bible, because of someone's past sin. Adultery causes so much pain and leads to so many problems and so many divorces. There are only two options if you catch your spouse in adultery:

1) Forgive and try to repair the relationship. It takes two people to repair a relationship.
2) Often time's one person is not willing to continue the relationship under any circumstances and divorce is the outcome. Even so forgiveness is essential for healing and you must forgive others so God can forgive you of any sins!

God hates divorce is what the bible says! There are many people in jail, because they chose other options like assault or murder. They have had jealous rages with lifelong consequences. "Vengeance is mine says the Lord."

Sometimes both parties are committing Adultery. It is a selfish act and usually destroys families. When people have an adulterous affair and then divorce for another, it usually never leads to another godly or healthy marriage. Eighty percent of second marriages fail because most start out of adultery. Is adultery sexual addiction? I think so.

It has been said many times that men have sex for physical reasons and woman for emotional reasons. I do not believe these are the only reasons. Maybe percentage-wise it is more physical for men but there are emotional reasons many times also. Woman, have physical reasons as well: it is not always just emotional. Both have physical and emotional reasons and it is just a different level for each gender. Sometimes this has been used by talk show hosts as justifications for adultery. Adultery is sin and there is no justification for it in the bible!

While writing this chapter in late 2009, a famous sports figure has made news headlines about his alleged numerous affairs. What is he in God's eyes? Many women are coming out of the woodwork to brag about it, or to try and profit from it. What are they in God's eyes? The news reported that he may have a sexual addiction. What was their first clue? Other blue ribbon panels on some liberal news channels are giving advice how to commit adultery and lessen the chance of getting caught! God still sees it all.

Some blame it on the wild women for the man's addiction. When a man joins to a woman in sexual union, the two become one: this is what the bible says not me. Probably one of the worst ways to have demonic oppression of lust come into your life is to engage in sex outside of marriage. When the Lord is your Shepherd, then the temptations are easier to face and turn away from.

Go now to the "Final Thoughts" section after the last chapter. Then read the sinner's prayer and make the Lord your Shepherd!

Recently I watched a documentary of the Woodstock music festival that was in 1969. People who had been there, and are now years older, were talking about how it was a "spiritual awakening". God was not in Woodstock, but Satan was. Lust permeated the air over the festival. Sexual addiction began to reach new levels after this event and during the "hippie" era in general.

Some musical lyrics glamorize fornication in obvious and subtle ways.

Musical lyrics should be listened to with caution when dealing with addictions. Many times they play into emotions that tend to encourage or enable the activity of the addiction. Once an addiction has been recognized, then old favorite songs should be avoided.

The world's liberal attitudes about sex have become the everyday norm. Our Christian ideals have been dwindling for years and sexual addictions have become normal behavior among all people. Men with extreme sexual addictions, such as pedophilia, will travel all over the world. The internet has not caused it, but has just created another avenue for this sub-culture to exist and communicate.

Abducting women and children, and holding them in sexual slavery goes on in many parts of the world. There have been many cases brought to national attention in the United States alone. A recent case of a child that had been abducted and held in slavery, in the back yard of a known sex offender for 17 years in California, was a terrible situation, and a sad day for law enforcement. How many people turned a blind eye to this or spoke up to deaf ears.

Many times it is a trusted person or person in authority who begins sexually abusing a child. Catholic priests had been molesting young boys for years, until it was brought out in numerous civil cases. The Catholic Church condemns homosexuals, adultery, and divorce, and in the past mostly turned a blind eye to pedophile priests. All male homosexuals are not child abusers but all men who sexually abuse young boys are homosexuals. Any homosexuals that are allowed to preach the Word of God by any denomination or congregation is a contradiction to the Word of God!

Homosexual behavior has come out of the closet and into the classrooms. There may be a very few people born with sexual deformities. Most men and women become addicted to homosexual behavior. Maybe they were influenced by a person or demonic spirit at some point in their life. Some were sexually abused in their childhood or hurt in a normal heterosexual relationship. Any of these could have led them into rebellion from God and into a homosexual lifestyle. Saying "I was born that way" is a common excuse for sin.

There is no such thing as gay marriage. The term "gay" is misleading as most all homosexuals are not truly happy and they cannot have true joy.

You will not be "gay" the day you kneel in front of the Lord. That statement is conviction not condemnation. The point here is that Jesus spoke out against homosexuals. Jesus said and I agree that people should not have hate towards them or harm them due to their lifestyle. God hates the sin not the person. Homosexuality is a sexual aberration and addiction. It is a sin according to the Word of God in the Bible.

There are so called "Christian" cults that promote everything from forced marriage, rape and/or child abuse. These groups are not Christians and are being led astray by evil men perverting God's Word. As said earlier, those who pervert the Word of God to commit sexual sin will answer to Him in the end. Just because there is a Christian lingo on a building does not make it a Christian church! Some claim to be Christians, but are not teaching what is biblical at all.

Bestiality is probably one of the most deranged forms of sexual addiction. There is a link between bestiality and sexual abuse of children as well as with serial rapists. There have been new laws passed in several areas to deal with this growing problem, because there were not any laws on the books in the past.

Probably the most highly addictive sexual addiction is pornography and exotic strippers. Sex sells is a favorite saying among sales people. I had listened to a news report several years ago where a woman said most of the porn industry was made up of men. What she was trying to say was it was controlled by men. Most of the industry consists of woman. These men prey on women and lure them to work in the porn industry. In turn these women seductively prey on men by offering them sexual services for money. Anyone who says this is a harmless industry and that it should be legalized is not speaking for God. Men are the ones who are most addicted, and it causes many emotional and spiritual problems with them and their families. It raises the chances for further sexual sins and addictions for all those involved. There is no such thing as sexual sin being "adult entertainment". Unless they repent, people that make, produce, or distribute porn have much to answer for when they kneel before the Lord.

How to solve this plague of porn throughout the world? Very simply, do not buy it, do not make it, and do not watch it! It is one industry that could easily dry up. All the money made, and all the guilt and remorse later in life, will not be worth the participation in it. When the Lord is your Shepherd and you read, believe, and understand the Word, then you will know the eternal consequences of pornography. Porn leads to many other sins and can encourage other addictions.

Go now to the "Final Thoughts" section after the last chapter. Then read the sinner's prayer and make the Lord your Shepherd!

The Lord may have been with you in places you should not have been during your addiction, but his hand of protection may not have been there. I consider this as a sheep going into a cave: the Shepherd may not be able to reach you there. Psalms 23:4 says "Yea, though I walk through the valley of the shadow of death, I will fear no evil; for You are with me; Your rod and Your staff, they comfort me." If you are in the midst of a sexual addiction, then you are flirting with disaster, or even possibly your eternity.

Not long before I retired a female prisoner asked for me. She had just returned from a required visit to the Health Department. She had the look of fear all over her face because they had told her she tested positive for HIV. She had three children and asked me to pray for her. Just prior to this my Pastor was giving a sermon on not being afraid to lay hands on sick people and to pray for them. I walk over to this lady and laid hands on her shoulder. She was trembling. We prayed and I told her what she needed to do spiritually. All the pleasure she had enjoyed was not worth the infirmity and fear the devil had brought into her life.

Only the Lord Jesus can fill the imaginary hole in your heart. Trying to fill it with anything else, or any addictions, is like trying to fill a bottomless pit.

There is no problem too big for God! When you make the Lord your Shepherd, then the power of these addictive spirits, become less of a problem to you. When a thought comes to your mind, you can say out loud, "I rebuke that spirit in the name of Jesus!" With that, demons must flee, and peace will enter your heart. Jesus said, "You shall know the truth, and the truth will make you free". This information is very powerful in the area of addictions. Destroy the addiction, and you will be freed from the sins that addictions present.

The Lord will not do what you can do for yourself. You have to take the key and lock the gate and with the help of the Lord destroy the addiction. The same key opens your heart to let the Lord inside to be your Shepherd, Savior, Deliverer, Healer, Provider and much more. You have to seek out scriptures in the Bible that pertain to you. Then you use those scriptures as ammunition when temptation comes at you. You can find them by using references, indexes or concordances for the Bible. Find a version you understand and cross reference your favorite scriptures to other versions. Then listen to the Word of God from Holy Spirit-filled pastors at a church, on Christian radio and television, or on tapes, CD or DVD's, or the internet. Faith comes by hearing and you can receive a new revelation every time you hear or read the Word of God.

Go now to the "Final Thoughts" section after the last chapter. Then read the sinner's prayer and make the Lord your Shepherd!

7

Spending

We have all heard that you cannot take it with you when you go (meaning when you die). Many people have bad spending habits. That is why the rich get richer, in most cases, and the regular folks and poor get poorer. When does a bad habit become an addiction? There are billions and billions of credit card debits at the time of writing this chapter in early 2010. For some people there is an addiction to buying things for instant gratification to fill their hearts. People buy for needs or just wanting nice things. Having nice things is ok if you can afford them, but to buy things to fill a void in your life, usually is a sign of an addiction.

Only the Lord Jesus can fill the imaginary hole in your heart. Trying to fill it with anything else, or any addictions, is like trying to fill a bottomless pit.

We have already discussed in this book alcohol, drugs, food, gambling and sex. If you stop and think about all the money spent on or associated with these things it is amazing. Alcohol, drugs, and tobacco (discussed in next chapter) are the perfect products to make lots of money. Once addicted, people just keep coming back and buying more.

Food is a need for everyone. When addicted to food then spending habits for food become an addiction. Sometimes people can be addicted to eating at restaurants all the time. They may never feed themselves at home and many times will run up the credit card because of their laziness. This habit becomes an addiction when you spend excessively, and are overweight from eating too much great tasting food prepared by others.

When buying non-addicting products to an extreme and you have no real use or need, then you probably have an addiction to spending. There are some people who have inherited or made lots of money that never tithe or give money to any needy cause. They fill their house up with "stuff". Sometimes you cannot walk through the house for boxes and boxes of "stuff". The garage, attic, basement, storage buildings and house are filled with "stuff". Some things have never been opened or taken out of the boxes. Having a collection of nice things is ok to a point, but spending constantly to buy things one does not need is an addiction. Spending addicts have to buy something to fill their hearts, when only the Lord can do this.

Everyone with a spending addiction may not fill their house up with boxes of things. Many women have closets full of clothes and shoes that they never wear. While many poor go without basic things, there are some shopping addicts who care only for themselves. This is call greed and is talked about in the bible.

When it is time for me to change seasonal clothes I become excited about finding things that I no longer like or can wear. They are gathered up and given to charity. I know deep inside, that there is someone who will need it more than I do. If you cannot even think about giving something away and have too much "stuff", then you probably have a spending addiction. If you are giving away things just to

PSALMS 23 "The Key to the Cure of all Addictions"

make room for more, then that is wasteful spending, and you probably have an addiction.

At this time there are so many scams to sell products. It can be a constant battle not to spend too much and to get the best price. It requires constantly using good judgment in buying items. When the Lord is your Shepherd then the Holy Spirit will guide you in making good decisions: you will have the favor of the Lord and will buy things that you need wisely. Many friends of mine over the years have asked me how I purchase things at such great prices. Many times I wait for sales if possible. Sometimes I will barter or just expect the favor of the Lord to fill my needs. I have purchased things and did not think I got a great deal, until I later realized the purchase was a good deal and blessing. Many times others have asked me to buy something from them that I need, in like new condition at a great price. That is the favor of God. Be a good steward with the money that passes through your hands: tithe, give offerings to the church and the needy. Then watch your life have more blessing than you can imagine.

Go now to the "Final Thoughts" section after the last chapter. Then read the sinner's prayer and make the Lord your Shepherd!

8

THEFT

Taking something that does not belong to you is stealing, anyway that you do it or try to justify it. God's commandment, "Thou Shall not Steal" is common knowledge to most people. To some stealing brings as much excitement as gambling. That is because stealing and gambling are related. It is the thrill of getting something for nothing. A petty thief who was an alcohol and drug addict told me, that stealing from the stores gave him a high as good as drugs or better. He said sometimes he even had the money to pay, but stole the item to get the high. If this is you, then you have a stealing addiction.

From the billionaire Ponzi schemers, to embezzlers, burglars, robbers, and petty thieves, it is all the same. Stealing is stealing! There are people in every walk of life and profession who steal: employees at stores, doctor's offices, government offices, investment firms, church offices, to mail and package delivery people, office workers, factory workers, restaurant workers, and even law enforcement and military personnel.

There are so many people in jail that have an addiction to stealing, which usually is associated to other addictions.

PSALMS 23 "The Key to the Cure of all Addictions"

There are some people that rarely have a job, and they just steal when they want or need things.

Many times, working as a police officer, I would calculate to people how much time they were going to spend in jail for the amount they stole. Let's say you broke into a house and stole jewelry then sold it for $20,000. Most thieves think that is a big catch. But then you are arrested and convicted and sent to jail for 10 years. You will spend each day of the 10 years in jail for $5.50! That does not seem like a great idea anymore. Now figure it on just 1000 years in hell. That works out to 5 cents a day for 1000 years! Although we know hell is for eternity. People have robbed stores at gun point and have stolen a mere $20, then went to jail for 10 years or have died trying. Others have stolen $20,000,000 and only got 10 years in jail. The amount of the theft really does not matter when talking about hell. Hell is a lot worse than any jail! The glamour of stealing from the movies will not matter in jail or hell. Remember hell is for eternity. That is forever and ever...

Maybe you have stolen very much, and it has gone undetected on this earth by people. But, it has not gone undetected by God. The first thing to do is stop, turn away from stealing, and repent. Then make the Lord your Shepherd. Do not think there is time later to repent.

Stealing is about wants most of the time. Stealing is based in spite and envy. There is no peace with stolen goods. You will bring curses on your house and family. It may be good for a time, but then there is a price to pay, even if not on this earth.

Go now to the "Final Thoughts" section after the last chapter. Then read the sinner's prayer and make the Lord your Shepherd!

Read Proverbs, Psalms and the Gospels of Matthew, Mark, Luke and John and the book of Acts. Concentrate on the red letters which are Jesus quotes, in the New Testament.

Jesus talked about money very much in the Bible and God put "Thou Shall not Steal" in one of the Ten Commandments for a reason. When you stop stealing and destroy the addiction, then any other addictions can be destroyed too.

9
TOBACCO

My brother once told me that tobacco is the perfect product: it is legal, and people keep coming back for more because they get addicted. It has a long history but has no real health value. There was a big debate in the 1960s and before over whether tobacco was harmful, or not. In the 1970s that debate really ended. People then believed that nicotine was not really a big deal. They believed all the warnings, talk and studies about the dangers of tobacco were exaggerated.

Nicotine is the addictive drug in tobacco, but not the only dangerous chemical. There are so many other chemicals that are harmful and dangerous to the human body in tobacco.

Most people do not start using tobacco when they are adults. Tobacco use for most people usually starts when they are teenagers. But the tobacco industry states that they do not advertise to young people: that is their official policy.

Remember that Cigarettes are a gateway drug and it can open the gate to more serious and harsher drugs. Many drug addicts told me they would have never used harder drugs if they had not used Alcohol, Marihuana and Cigarettes first!

The tobacco industry is not as concerned about the market in the United States, since there's been an increase in lawsuits etc... They have now turned their attention to third world countries. While working in Iraq for 15 months and traveling to the Philippines this became apparent to me. Most Iraqi Police that I talked to while training (through interpreters) did not even know that smoking was harmful. It was really sad for me to see all the young men in Iraq and the Philippines smoking and not knowing the dangers of tobacco. While there I realized the huge markets for tobacco in many other third world countries, as well.

The tobacco industry is based on greed, as is the drug industry. Millions of people are starving all over the world, and tobacco growers are using good land to grow a product that has no human value. Tobacco growers in the United States are now polluting other countries with tobacco products. Now this statement may seem harsh to many people, but it is true.

The long term effects of smoking or chewing tobacco is no secret. Smoking causes many physical illnesses from heart and lung disease and cancer to cataract. Heart disease is called the silent killer. I did not understand the term silent killer before. Then I listened to a report on how many times there are no symptoms to heart disease. Not like lung problems where you can cough and be sick for years. With the heart it can hit with no warning.

In November 2009 at a hunting club, I learned this first hand. The day before the season opened, I went there to scout around. At sunset I returned to our cabin, and another member pulled up in his truck. We had met years before but did not know each other. We introduced ourselves, and he unloaded his hunting gear. We then cleaned up the cabin, and ate some leftovers. He was a very nice and friendly man of about 60 years of age. He also appeared to be in fair health, not overweight or frail looking. As we talked, he finished

PSALMS 23 "The Key to the Cure of all Addictions"

washing the dishes, turned off the water, lifted his arms up, and his head tilted back. This man had a massive heart attack. I called for an ambulance, did CPR, and it took 20 minutes for the ambulance to get there, because we were far out in the country. He did not live. I found out later he was still a smoker, and had previously had open heart surgery. His life was cut short by the use of tobacco. Some people will say "Well, you've got to go sometime." I do not think he wanted to go that night. He was planning on many things the next day and in the future.

Smoking tobacco is a constant cycle of temporary enjoyment and destruction of the body. It is an acquired habit that is not enjoyable at first. In the late 1970s some of the tobacco industries began spiking nicotine levels. This made it more difficult for people to quit.

There are all kinds of programs to quit tobacco use and there are even prescription drugs available. The way I quit back in 1977, was using what a friend told me to do. She said "Quit cold turkey, and don't buy them or bum them, and do not drink (alcohol) for a week." Many people quit, then drink alcohol, and go right back to smoking. Quitting both tobacco and alcohol at the same time would be the best solution.

Go now to the "Final Thoughts" section after the last chapter. Then read the sinner's prayer and make the Lord your Shepherd!

Maybe you have accepted the Lord as you Savior but never have allowed him to be you Shepherd. When you make the Lord your Shepherd and lay down your tobacco addiction, He will help you destroy it. You have to do your part. Any program or medicine that helps you quit tobacco is great, but any medicine should only be used for a short time. (Some have replaced a tobacco habit with smoking more marihuana-Not a good idea!)

People who only chew tobacco think they are not at such a high risk as those who smoke. This may be true for some diseases. You are still at a risk of other diseases. Mouth cancer and gum diseases, are just a few. It is still addictive and really a nasty habit. Just ask anyone who has to empty the trash can where chewing tobacco is discarded, whether in the work place or your home!

When I was in high school back in the 1970's, we were allowed to smoke outside the building, as did many other high schools around the country. I suppose they gave up enforcing "no smoking" in schools in the 1960s, when many were smoking in the boy's room. I remember when I quit, just before graduation in 1977, and I finally realized how dumb I looked when I smoked. It was sixty cents a pack when I quit and that was a waste of money even then.

During the 1980s most schools around the country began to enforce the "No Smoking" Policy. At my 25 class reunion, I was really shocked that most of the women were still smoking. I remembered thinking that it was really great that I had quit in 1977.

While riding the 2007 Cheaha Challenge on my bicycle, I was praying out loud going up a steep hill. I was thanking the Lord that I quit smoking. A man rode up next to me and asked me what I was doing? I told him I was thanking the Lord that I had quit smoking 30 years ago. He stated that he had quit 20 years ago. We both agreed that we would not be able to ride the 88 mile course if we still smoked.

I still encourage people who smoke to quit, no matter how long they have smoked. I try to do so with a kind and caring attitude. It is a difficult addiction to destroy. A famous rock star said on TV, that he had quit alcohol, cocaine, and heroin, but tobacco was the hardest to quit. That really is a powerful statement.

Many foods, vitamins and supplements are said to be antioxidants. Many are good to help eliminate toxins. Using tobacco adds more toxins to the body, which may not be eliminated and creates more health problems. Give this

PSALMS 23 "The Key to the Cure of all Addictions"

addiction over to the Lord. Use whatever method you find to quit tobacco. When the addiction is destroyed, then you can see the power in the Lord as your Shepherd. Healing can only really begin for tobacco related illnesses when you stop using tobacco. If you are not healed instantly then do not be discouraged, because it may take time. Never say it is too late to quit. You are only fooling yourself if you say I quit later.

The Lord will not do what you can do for yourself. You have to take the key and lock the gate and with the help of the Lord destroy the addiction. The same key opens your heart to let the Lord inside to be your Shepherd, Savior, Deliverer, Healer, Provider and much more. You have to seek out scriptures in the Bible that pertain to you. Then you use those scriptures as ammunition when temptation comes at you. You can find them by using references, indexes or concordances for the Bible. Find a version you understand and cross reference your favorite scriptures to other versions. Then listen to the Word of God from Holy Spirit-filled pastors at a church, on Christian radio and television, or on tapes, CD or DVD's, or the internet. Faith comes by hearing and you can receive a new revelation every time you hear or read the Word of God.

Go now to the "Final Thoughts" section after the last chapter. Then read the sinner's prayer and make the Lord your Shepherd!

10

VIOLENCE

    Satan and his demons, are roaming the earth, constantly searching for those they can destroy. Jesus said the devil is the father of all lies and comes like a thief to steal, kill, and destroy. The devil tempts and pushes and entices people that are angry to commit acts of violence. "The devil made me do it" is not possible unless you allow the devil or a demon to possess you. These evil people are addicted to violence. Christians cannot be possessed by the demons but can be oppressed. The devil and or demons cannot read your mind, but they can hear and see your words. The devil will then speak to your inner ear or through other people.

    Anger begets anger. Anger is one step away from danger. It is usually built up gradually, and often stems from past events. Anger can be a response from things not going your way, which is many times selfishness or disappointment.

    Jesus taught about controlled anger and violence. In the bible it says, to anger and do not sin. This is very difficult if you do not know Jesus as your Lord. Jesus did not say you cannot defend yourself from an act of violence. Many people have taken the commandment "Thou shall not kill." to an extreme, believing you cannot harm an evil violent person

PSALMS 23 "The Key to the Cure of all Addictions"

who attacks you or serve in the military. This has been said by foolish people ignorant of the Word of God. It is "Thou shall not kill." as in murder. Turning the other cheek is about minor things like a slap on the face or a verbal attack.

People that go on violent rampages and mentally snap usually have been planning out a violent act in their mind. They may never have committed an act of violence, but they have become addicted to it by playing things out in their minds. Just because you are tempted does not mean you have sinned. Thoughts proceeds action and when you know in your heart you are going to commit a violent act, then that is where the sins begin. It is better to stop the battle in your mind and turn away, then commit the act. Most of the time people that go on rampages do it because of anger from past emotional hurts or things they dreamed up in their minds. These are all lies of the devil. Many times people that have no connection to them become victims just by being in the wrong place during one of these rampages. Often the murderer commits suicide at the end of the rampage and suicide was their plan from the beginning. Where will the murderer end up? Will they be in a better place? Suicide is always a permanent solution to a temporary problem and never the answer, or way out, for anyone.

Go now to the "Final Thoughts" section after the last chapter. Then read the sinner's prayer and make the Lord your Shepherd!

In Proverbs it is written to trust in the Lord with **all** your heart. Do not try to understand everything. When you trust in people with **all** your heart then you will be very disappointed. When you try to figure out all the events in the world, your workplace, or in your government, then frustration will surely follow. Expectation in people, animals, or the weather is premeditated disappointment. You can expect good things from God, but maybe not in your timing.

In the Bible there was a man named "Jabez". He prayed for God to bless him, enlarge his territory, and keep God's protection over him. Then he makes a very powerful statement: he asks God to keep him from evil, that he may not cause pain. Think of all the ways that pain is caused by words, actions or violence.

Revenge has been around since the beginning of mankind. The Bible states, "Vengeance is mine, I will repay says the Lord". Let the Lord repay for past wrongs. God will judge in the end. When you commit evil acts of violence for revenge, then you make yourself a god. An old saying is "pay back is hell." Do you want to spend an eternity in hell for an act of revenge? Many people want to have the last word or final say by committing an act of violence. God was in the beginning and will be at the end. God will always have the last word or final say.

In some cultures, it is acceptable to commit an act of vengeance for something that happened thousands of years ago. Vengeance is a lie from the devil! God can handle any problem. If you think God did not judge or handle a problem that took place a thousand years ago, then you are thinking foolishly. Anger begets anger, and planning an act of violent revenge, becomes a powerful addiction.

Many extremists and terrorist groups are based on vengeance from hatred and different religious or political beliefs. Many times things are dreamed up in the minds of their leaders (through Satan's influence) and they mislead their followers, who become addicted to violence. These evil people often times go on murder/suicide missions.

Nowhere in the Bible does Jesus say you will enter Paradise by committing acts of violence and revenge. Every tongue will confess and every knee will one day bow to Jesus. Everyone will believe in Jesus Christ: do not wait until your judgment, and it is too late. Anyone that thinks they will have a special place with Satan after this life will be very surprised in hell.

Go now to the "Final Thoughts" section after the last chapter. Then read the sinner's prayer and make the Lord your Shepherd!

Evil dictators of countries have been possessed or seriously oppressed by the devil. Satan has used people in authority to commit acts of violence against innocent people. These rulers are addicted to violence, and feed it to their followers. Violence is used for power and control. Not all the people will buy into it, but some will be too oppressed by their leaders or Satan to exit the situation.

The evil dictators in history have been used by the devil to do his work, and have used a whole country instead of a few persons or an individual. Many people may be blind to their dictator's evil ways, just as they are blind to the devils ways. Once these dictators pass away, then God will deal with them. Any leader of a country or person in authority will be judged in the end. They have much more to answer for than the average person.

There are many people all over the world who have extreme views and are very angry over issues. They band together, dress up in uniforms and costumes or blend in with society. They organize militias, cults, or so called religious groups and have very violent attitudes. They breed anger amongst themselves, and recruit people that are like-minded and very angry. They believe that violence is a means to an end. They may profess peace, but in actuality, they breed violence. These extremists exist in every race, and have used the name of every religion.

Many criminals, gangs and organized crime groups have used violence to rob victims or attack other groups, committing acts of violence or vengeance. As always, their leaders breed anger with half-truths or lies, to the members in the group, and get them to perform the acts of violence. Many are paid, or rewarded, to carry out the acts. These people have a serious addiction to violence. If caught by authorities, the one committing the act of violence is the one to pay the heavy price. The prisons are full of these individuals. Some of these groups have an organized structure and plan things out very well. Their leaders many times have a plan to keep themselves distant from the one committing the act of violence.

There is no such thing as "getting away with murder" in God's eyes. In the end, all those involved will be judged. Many people who commit these acts have other forms of addictions. This is one reason they are so easily manipulated. You will stand alone for what you have done on this earth in the end.

Where is the fine line someone crosses to becoming addicted to violence? "When did this become a problem?" "Why did this happen to me?" "How did I let this get out of control?"

All violence begins in the mind with a thought or thoughts. The most dangerous weapon any person, criminal, or terrorist has is their mind. Some may carry their thoughts and plans around for years. Others may commit an act of violence spontaneously, after one initial thought precedes the violent act. Either way, all unnecessary acts of violence begin with thoughts of revenge.

The above paragraph applies to domestic violence also. Many cases of domestic violence are planned out for a long time. Some violence may just happen over an emotional incident. It never solves anything and only makes a situation worse. Many times it is over selfishness, spite, envy, greed, adultery or jealousy. Some of it is real, and many times it is imagined. If one spouse is committing adultery then the only two biblical things to do is:

PSALMS 23 "The Key to the Cure of all Addictions"

1) Forgive and try to repair the relationship. It takes two people to repair a relationship.
2) Often time's one person is not willing to continue the relationship under any circumstances and divorce is the outcome. Even so forgiveness is essential for healing and you must forgive others so God can forgive you!

Peaceful separation applies to domestic partners who are living outside of God's will already. Committing an act of violence is not the solution to the problem.

Many people are sitting in jail for years, for a crime of passion. Was there an addiction to violence? Did they have a violence addiction already? Most probably had anger problems and reacted violently without thinking of the consequences.

Referring to violence as an addiction is by no means justifying the act. Do not dwell on thoughts of violence because of past emotional hurts and pain. Putting **all** your hope and trust into another person will result in disappointment.

Only the Lord Jesus can fill the imaginary hole in your heart. Trying to fill it with revenge, is like trying to fill a bottomless pit.

Maybe you have never committed an act of violence, but have been dwelling on it for a time. Maybe you are involved in a lifestyle where violence is used occasionally. Maybe you have a full blown addiction to violence.

There is no problem too big for God! When you make the Lord your Shepherd, then the power of these addictive spirits, become less of a problem to you. When a thought comes to your mind, you can say out loud, "I rebuke that spirit in the name of Jesus!" With that, demons must flee, and peace will enter your heart. Jesus said, "You shall know the truth, and the truth will make you free". This information is very powerful in the area of addictions. Destroy the addiction, and you will be freed from the sins that addictions present.

Even if you give your life to the Lord and are forgiven of your violent sins (as Paul was) there may still be a price to pay on earth to fellow man. If you are sitting in a jail cell now, then you can still have spiritual freedom.

Go now to the "Final Thoughts" section after the last chapter. Then read the sinner's prayer and make the Lord your Shepherd!

There is also major problem with young people playing realistic, violent video games and becoming desensitized to violence. A military expert claims we are programming our youth to violent tendencies before a mature age. Could this lead to a violence addiction? The youth and young adults that spend a lot of time playing these type games are missing out on socialization skills, outdoor activities, and education for their future. There is nothing wrong with having fun with video games, but excessive amounts and violent games could be hazardous to your emotional health.

Stated earlier in this chapter was "The most dangerous weapon is the mind."! Violence has been committed with all kinds of items or objects, and these acts all started with a thought or an idea. Terrorist have used jet airplanes, bombs, chemicals or any weapon of mass destruction. Criminals and deranged people have used knives, swords, ball bats, hammers and any homemade item to commit violent acts. When someone uses a gun to commit an act of violence, many people in all walks of life will often speak out against the object: the gun. Their solution is to do away with guns, rather than addressing the anger and violence issue. Sometimes possible victims have needed to use a gun in self-defense towards a violent person. Guns are needed to protect the innocent.

There was violence before the gun was invented and there will be violence after the gun is obsolete. Either way violence will continue until the Lord returns, because it is a product of several worldly sins: spite, envy, anger, pride, selfishness and revenge to name a few. And, these are all evidence of a world where Satan is the only god that many today know.

After all it is a battle between good and evil. God is good and in the end, Jesus is all that matters. Go in peace.

Final Thoughts

Pray this out loud!

Sinners Prayer:
"Lord Jesus, come into my life. Forgive me of all my sins. I ask you to cleanse my heart, and make me a new person. I believe that you are the Son of God and that you died on the cross for my sins. Thank you for loving me enough to die for me. Please be the Lord of my life, and accept me just as I am. You are now my God, and I am your child. You are my Savior and my Lord.
    I Praise you in Jesus Name; Amen.

Thank You for reading my first book. God has blessed me so much. May God bless you when you draw near to him! I do not plan on doing book signings, tours or interviews. The author wishes to remain anonymous. This book is not about me. It is about your relationship with God the Father, Jesus and the Holy Spirit. You have to go to the Father only through Jesus. Remember the wages of sin is physical and spiritual death. Begin a relationship with Jesus and live now and forever.

PSALMS 23 "The Key to the Cure of all Addictions"

The Lord will not do what you can do for yourself. You have to take the key and lock the gate and with the help of the Lord destroy the addiction. The same key opens your heart to let the Lord inside to be your Shepherd, Savior, Deliverer, Healer, Provider and much more. You have to seek out scriptures in the Bible that pertain to you. Then you use those scriptures as ammunition when temptation comes at you. You can find them by using references, indexes or concordances for the Bible. Find a version you understand and cross reference your favorite scriptures to other versions. Then listen to the Word of God from Holy Spirit-filled pastors at a church, on Christian radio and television, or on tapes, CD or DVD's, or the internet. Faith comes by hearing and you can receive a new revelation every time you hear or read the Word of God.

This book has tried to explain why Psalms 23 is "The Key to the Cure of all Addictions". You open the door to your heart and allow Jesus inside. An old saying I love is; "If at first you don't succeed then read the directions". The Bible is our direction manual.

God is the same yesterday, today and tomorrow. God's Word is living and every time you hear or read the Word, you may receive a new revelation for your life.

I cannot thank my pastor Michael Cox enough, for all his great biblical teaching at Cornerstone Worship Center. A very special thanks to Karen (Barnwell) Tierce and Tonya Love, who painstakingly proof read the drafts and corrected my grammar. Tonya, Thank you so much for encouraging me to finish this book!

Hopefully you have found or will find the Key and accept Jesus as your Lord, Savior and Shepherd. Then you can destroy your addiction. Maybe you are still on your way. Once you have destroyed your addiction then help others find the Key. Encourage them in a loving way. Your actions speak louder than your words. Many people that were hard on you about your addictions may have their own addictions. Their addictions may be different than yours and they see no problem with their addiction. Many people you know or that come across your path will suffer from addictions. Plant seeds of the Word of God in them. Do this in an encouraging, enlightening and loving way. Talk of the benefits of destroying and eliminating addictions. There is still a time for tough love. Show them the Key or give them a copy of this book.

Never accept abusive or offensive remarks from anyone you talk to about Jesus. If they get angry, they will cool off. Do not feel guilty. You do not have to defend God. Just remember how you felt and reacted when people approached you about your addiction. God Bless and remember in the end all that really matters is the Lord Jesus Christ!

Kevin St. John

Positive comments can be sent to: Kevstjohn@aol.com

For more information contact: http://cwcchurch.com/
Or write: Cornerstone Worship Center
              2885 Choccolocco Road
              Anniston, Alabama 36207
Phone: (256) 236-1603

www.ingramcontent.com/pod-product-compliance
Ingram Content Group UK Ltd.
Pitfield, Milton Keynes, MK11 3LW, UK
UKHW041948230426
12048UKWH00008B/216